COUNTING THE DAYS

UNDENIABLE SIGNS OF THE LAST DAYS

RAY COMFORT

BRIDGE
LOGOS

Newberry, FL 32669

Counting the Days:
Undeniable Signs of the Last Days

Bridge-Logos, Inc.
Newberry, FL 32669, USA

ISBN 978-1-610362-54-2

Library of Congress Control Number: 2020947715

Edited by Lynn Copeland

Cover by Jeremey Wilson

Page design and layout by Genesis Group

Cartoons by Richard Gunther

Printed in the United States of America

Reprinted February 2021

CONTENTS

INTRODUCTION

THOSE WHO KNOW their Bible know that we are seeing many biblical prophecies unfolding before our eyes, and as I've watched these "signs of the times" come to pass, I have been reminded about the way the apostle Paul shared the gospel:

> So when they had appointed him a day, many came to [Paul] at his lodging, to whom he explained and solemnly testified of the kingdom of God, *persuading them concerning Jesus from both the Law of Moses and the Prophets*, from morning till evening. (Acts 28:23)

When he spoke about Jesus, he *persuaded* unbelievers "from both the Law of Moses and the prophets." The Law of Moses brings the knowledge of sin (showing us our danger), and the prophets give credibility to the Scriptures. In other words, if the Bible is able to predict the future, it is evidence that it was written by the hand of our omniscient Creator. Those who penned its pages did so under the inspiration of Almighty God.

This is because only *He* knows the end from the beginning. And if the Bible *is* the Word of God, its promise of everlasting life is both sure and steadfast. It's an anchor for the human soul. We can have a living hope in our death.

If you want to spark some disagreement, tell someone what you believe the Scriptures say about a certain prophetic event. It is because of this potential to cause division that I have looked only at mainstream prophetic interpretations. My hope in doing this is that you will feel comfortable passing this book on to those who don't believe because they don't have this knowledge.

CHAPTER ONE

HOW TO KNOW THE FUTURE

I MAKE KNOWN
THE END FROM
THE BEGINNING
FROM ANCIENT
TIMES

GEORGE ORWELL WROTE, "If you want a picture of the future, imagine a boot stamping on a human face—for ever."

Such were the pessimistic words of one of the characters in his famous novel *1984*, where he predicted the future.

Published in 1949, the bestselling book centers on the consequences of totalitarianism, mass surveillance, and repressive regimentation of all persons and behaviors within society. But 1984 came and went. It's now history. Though Orwell's character was bold in his predictions, with the continued international tensions after the Second World War it wasn't too difficult to predict that the human face would continue to be stomped upon. Predicting that tomorrow's news will be bad isn't exactly newsworthy.

There are a number of ways human beings can know the future. We know that if we throw a rock in

the air, it will certainly come down. Eventually. We know that if we jump into the ocean, we will get wet, and if we leap off a high cliff, we will die. If we don't eat, hunger waits around the corner. And as long as there are nations, there will be wars. Each of those futures is merely consequential.

There are also weather forecasters, political pundits, and financial experts who use data to attempt to predict the future, but they are often wrong. That's predictable.

There is another way we can "know the future." It's to have knowledge of something that has already happened. When Sue and I want to watch our favorite rugby team, we always check the final score first before we watch the recorded game on video. While not knowing the outcome is part of the excitement for most, knowing how it ends means that we don't stress when the other side scores. And stress is not good at our age. When the opponent scores a goal and the crowd exchanges high-fives, we smile because we know the outcome. There's no stress.

In reality, if human beings could see even one minute into the future, we could make billions by sitting at a high-roller table in Las Vegas because we would know where to put our chips. But we don't.

However, there is one light among the future's darkness. The Bible is filled with prophecy; in fact, more than one-fourth of its pages contain predictive prophecy, all of which has come true in the smallest detail. From its opening chapters, God Himself tells us what will happen:

> "And I will put enmity
> Between you and the woman,
> And between your seed and her Seed;
> He shall bruise your head,
> And you shall bruise His heel." (Genesis 3:15)

From this promise to avenge humanity's fall into sin and death, to the book of Revelation—where it speaks of great plagues that would cover the whole earth (see Revelation 16)—there are thousands of prophecies. In these and the many others between them, God is the one giving the prophecy, speaking through prophets. Again, only He knows the future.

Before we look at these amazing predictions, I want us to do something very important. I would like to expand our view of God. A man can look at a small portion of the Grand Canyon and boast that he has *seen* the Grand Canyon. But in reality, he's seen only a small part. Most of us have a *measured* belief in God, but because we are human beings, our understanding is very limited. It's small. We see a mere speck—and somehow we think we have seen it all, when God is nothing like we imagine Him to be.

To try to dash these erroneous images, we will take a moment to look at a tiny speck of the Creator's creation: you.

There are at least two things in life that I know my brain can't handle. The first is when two people begin talking to me at once. I don't think I'm alone in that. The other is when numbers get too big for me to comprehend. I tend to switch off at a certain point.

Take, for example, the thought that scientists estimate your body contains about 70 trillion cells. That's a big number, but I can handle it. It tells me that there are a *lot* of cells in the human body.

Then, according to an estimate made by engineers at Washington University, there are around 100 trillion atoms in a typical human cell.[1] That's a big number, but I can handle that also.

This is where I become overwhelmed. If there are (approximately) 70 trillion cells that make up your body, and each cell contains 100 trillion atoms, that means your body is composed of 70 trillion times 100 trillion atoms. Therefore, to create you, God made and correctly put together, in their precise placements, an estimated 7,000,000,000,000, 000,000,000,000,000 atoms.

It's not the size of the *number* that confounds me. It's my ability to comprehend what that number represents. I feel like a flea trying to comprehend the size of the universe while sitting on a dog's wagging tail. It's beyond my giddy flea-brain.

Here now is my point. God used atoms as building blocks to create you. He began this at your conception, and as time passed and you grew in size, He preprogrammed your genes to automatically add atoms at the right time and in the right places, until you reach physical maturity. *And*, because He is omniscient, He is intimately familiar with *every* single atom in your body, *and* in the bodies of every human being ever born, as well as every atom in everything in the entire universe—because He created every one of them.

But there's more. Have you ever noticed that God seems to have used a similar blueprint for the creation of many living creatures? Whether it's pigs, dogs, horses, cats, cows, or fish, He has made them all with a skeletal frame, one brain, one mouth, two eyes, and one heart to pump red blood around the body. He made human beings uniquely in His image, but much of creation seems to have been given these common characteristics.

I say "seems" because there is one amazing animal that sounds like it's a weird space alien, concocted by crazed minds in a cheaply produced Hollywood movie. This creature has an incredible *nine* brains, *three* pumping hearts, *eight* arms, no bones at all in its entire body, and *blue* blood.

The octopus (of which there are around 300 species) blows any preconceptions we may have about God out of the water. His creative ability knows no bounds. With Him, *nothing* is impossible.

Divine Identity

We are soon going to look at some of the Bible's prophecies, many of which were spoken directly by Jesus. I would therefore like to establish His credentials (according to the Bible) to give credibility to His amazing words.

The intellectual giddiness doesn't stop with the magnitude of God's creative ability. It becomes more intense as we consider the miracle of what is commonly referred to as the "incarnation."

Two thousand years ago, the Creator used trillions of atoms to make one unique human body for Himself. He was born on earth as Jesus of Nazareth. When He came into the world, He said:

> "Sacrifice and offering You did not desire, *but a body You have prepared for Me*." (Hebrews 10:5)

Then He filled that human body with Himself:

> And without controversy great is the mystery of godliness:

> God was manifested in the flesh, Justified in the Spirit,

Seen by angels,
Preached among the Gentiles,
Believed on in the world,
Received up in glory. (1 Timothy 3:16)

God became a very special Man—Jesus Christ.
Then the Scriptures tell us that every single atom in
every human body, and the universe, was actually
made by this Jesus:

In the beginning was the Word, and the
Word was with God, and the Word was God.
He was in the beginning with God. *All things
were made through Him, and without Him
nothing was made that was made*...And the
Word became flesh and dwelt among us, and
we beheld His glory, the glory as of the only
begotten of the Father, full of grace and
truth. (John 1:1–3,14)

He has delivered us from the power of darkness and conveyed us into the kingdom of
the Son of His love, in whom we have redemption through His blood, the forgiveness
of sins.
He is the image of the invisible God, the
firstborn over all creation. For by Him all
things were created that are in heaven and that
are on earth, visible and invisible, whether
thrones or dominions or principalities or
powers. *All things were created through Him
and for Him.* And He is before all things, and
in Him all things consist. (Colossians 1:15–17)

Then add to this mind-blowing thought that He became human flesh for the purpose of suffering and dying on the cross, so that we could be free from death. It is then that even the intellectually astute give up trying to comprehend our Creator and instead bow the knee in humble worship.

If you can't do that just yet, my hope is that the subject of prophecy will get you there, as we begin to look at what the Bible tells us about the past and the future.

CHAPTER TWO

THE TAROT READER

SAM, OUR BICHON, sat quietly on the platform I'd made for him on my bicycle. Looking very cool wearing his yellow sunglasses, he was my "bait" when I went fishing for men. Many times I had boldly ridden right up to strangers knowing the immediate future. They would predictably say, "Hey, I like your dog!" I would then hand them a card with his picture on it and say, "It's a YouTube channel with over 130,000,000 views. I ask people if there is an afterlife. What do you think? Where do people go when they die?" When they gave their thoughts, I would ask them if they would like to do an interview, and more often than not they would.

But as I sat on my bike on a sidewalk this day at a local park, it wasn't working. A gentlemen, perhaps in his late twenties, was reading a book and

9

wearing earbuds. Three times I had loudly said, "Excuse me," to no avail. I thought he was perhaps deliberately ignoring me, until he finally looked up and smiled as he saw Sam. Then I went through my routine.

It worked, and a few minutes later I was sitting at a picnic table in front of him. He was very friendly, and as we made small talk I looked down and saw a mass of cards on the table. When I asked what they were, he said they were tarot cards. My heart leaped with joy because, a few minutes earlier, I had determined to talk about Bible prophecy with the next person I interviewed.

Josh was a little skeptical about how many views our YouTube channel had, so I had to sit and wait as he looked it up to confirm what I told him. I then began recording and said, "I'm going to have to get your permission to interview you. Is that okay?" He said it was, so I framed him, lifted up the microphone and asked, "Josh, may I have permission to interview you for YouTube and for all media purposes?" He agreed, so I began with a question. Here is a transcript of that colorful conversation:

RAY: What are you doing?

JOSH: I'm studying tarot right now.

RAY: Studying *what*?

JOSH: Tarot.

RAY: What's that?

JOSH: Tarot is a very old cartomancy [fortunetelling by interpreting playing cards]. People reading cards came from the Gypsies, and they tried to discern either the future or people's past.

RAY: Is it working?

JOSH: For me it is because I'm just trying to see what's deeper in my mind and in the mind of others. I'm not really trying to read the future or anything.

RAY: Do you think people know the future?

JOSH: I think people can *predict* it pretty well.

RAY: I think there's a difference between predicting [and knowing]. When the weather forecast is predicted, they have a certain amount of knowledge and information and they say, "I *think* this will happen," but many a parade has been rained upon because the weather forecasters got it wrong. And if people could *really* predict the future— even ten minutes, five minutes— they'd go to Las Vegas and predict what's going to happen on the gambling table and make millions of dollars. So, it's pretty hard to know the future.

Have you ever studied *biblical* prophecy?

JOSH: No, not really.

RAY: Have you ever studied Nostradamus?

JOSH: No.

RAY: Nostradamus was into the darker side, and he predicted the future and he often got it right. You know why?

JOSH: Because he could read the signs?

RAY: No. He read his Bible in secret, ripped off Bible prophecies, and said they were his own. So, anyone who's ignorant of Bible prophecies thinks Nostradamus is really good.

Have you ever studied the scientific facts in the Bible?

JOSH: No.

RAY: The Bible has lots of scientific facts, like it says that the world hangs upon nothing—it speaks of the free float in space. It speaks of the *circle* of the earth—the earth being circular. It speaks of quarantining, two or three thousand years before man discovered if you've got a contagious disease you're supposed to quarantine. Lots of stuff like that, and then there's biblical *prophecies*. Do you know any of the signs of the end of the age?

JOSH: No.

RAY: Well, it says there will be wars and rumors of wars; there will be earthquakes, and famines, and diseases. It says Jerusalem would be in the hands of non-Jewish people "until the times of the Gentiles are fulfilled." In other words, the Jews would get Jerusalem back—and that happened in 1967. For the first time in two thousand years the Jews got Jerusalem back.

[I was encouraged that Josh was listening so intently. I didn't give him the details of what the Bible says about Jerusalem, but I will give them to you so that you can see how clearly the Scriptures lay out the future —for those who are interested.]

Blind Guides

Look at the scathing words of Jesus in Matthew 23, as He speaks to religious hypocrites telling them that, because of unrepentant sin, judgment would fall upon Jerusalem. As you read His words, notice how He speaks as God when He says, "*I* send you prophets..." Throughout the Old Testament, *Jesus* sent prophets to His people to call them to repentance.

"Blind guides, who strain out a gnat and swallow a camel!

"Woe to you, scribes and Pharisees, hypocrites! For you cleanse the outside of the cup and dish, but inside they are full of extortion and self-indulgence. Blind Pharisee, first cleanse the inside of the cup and dish, that the outside of them may be clean also.

"Woe to you, scribes and Pharisees, hypocrites! For you are like whitewashed tombs which indeed appear beautiful outwardly, but inside are full of dead men's bones and all uncleanness. Even so you also outwardly appear righteous to men, but inside you are full of hypocrisy and lawlessness.

"Woe to you, scribes and Pharisees, hypocrites! Because you build the tombs of the prophets and adorn the monuments of the righteous, and say, 'If we had lived in the days of our fathers, we would not have been partakers with them in the blood of the prophets.'

"Therefore you are witnesses against yourselves that you are sons of those who murdered the prophets. Fill up, then, the measure of your fathers' guilt. Serpents, brood of vipers! How can you escape the condemnation of hell? *Therefore, indeed, I send you prophets*, wise men, and scribes: some of them you will kill and crucify, and some of them you will scourge in your synagogues and persecute from city to city, that on you may come all the righteous blood shed on the earth, from the blood of righteous Abel to the blood of Zechariah, son of Berechiah, whom you murdered between the temple and the altar. Assuredly, I say to you, all these things will come upon this generation. (Matthew 23:24–36)

Jesus then addressed the horrific judgment that would come upon the city of Jerusalem, and in doing so He again speaks as God in saying, "How often I wanted to gather your children together…":

"O Jerusalem, Jerusalem, the one who kills the prophets and stones those who are sent to her! *How often I wanted to gather your children together*, as a hen gathers her chicks under her wings, but you were not willing! See! Your house is left to you desolate…" (Matthew 23:37,38)

Here is what Jesus specifically said about the future of Jerusalem, from the Gospel of Luke:

"But when you see Jerusalem surrounded by armies, then know that its desolation is near. Then let those who are in Judea flee to the mountains, let those who are in the midst of her depart, and let not those who are in the country enter her. For these are the days of vengeance, that all things which are written may be fulfilled. But woe to those who are pregnant and to those who are nursing babies in those days! For there will be great distress in the land and wrath upon this people. And they will fall by the edge of the sword, and be led away captive into all nations. And

Jerusalem will be trampled by Gentiles until the times of the Gentiles are fulfilled." (Luke 21:20–24)

Bible scholars believe that this foretells the historically well-documented destruction of Jerusalem in AD 70. *Encyclopaedia Britannica* said of it:

In April 70 [AD], about the time of Passover, the Roman general Titus besieged Jerusalem. Since that action coincided with Passover, the Romans allowed pilgrims to enter the city but refused to let them leave—thus strategically depleting food and water supplies within Jerusalem. Within the walls, the Zealots, a militant anti-Roman party, struggled with other Jewish factions that had emerged, which weakened the resistance even more. Josephus, a Jew who had commanded rebel forces but then defected to the Roman cause, attempted to negotiate a settlement, but, because he was not trusted by the Romans and was despised by the rebels, the talks went nowhere. The Romans encircled the city with a wall to cut off supplies to the city completely and thereby drive the Jews to starvation.[2]

At the beginning of this prophecy, Matthew says,

Then Jesus went out and departed from the temple, and His disciples came up to show Him the buildings of the temple. And Jesus said to them, "Do you not see all these things? Assuredly, I say to you, not one stone shall be left here upon another, that shall not be thrown down." (Matthew 24:1,2)

Notice the specificity of His words—that not one stone shall be left on another. One Bible commentator wrote:

d. **Not one stone shall be left here upon another:** Some 40 years after Jesus said this, there was a widespread Jewish revolution against the Romans in Palestine, and they enjoyed many early successes. But ultimately Roman soldiers crushed the rebels. In AD 70 Jerusalem was leveled, including the temple— just as Jesus said would happen.

i. "Titus (it is said) would have preserved the temple, as one of the world's wonders, from being burnt, but could not; such was the fury of his soldiers, set a-work by God doubtless." (Trapp)

ii. It is said that at the fall of Jerusalem, the last surviving Jews of the city fled to the temple, because it was the strongest and most secure building in the city. Roman soldiers surrounded it, and one drunken soldier started a fire that soon engulfed the whole building. Ornate gold detail work in the roof melted down in the cracks between the stone walls of the temple, and to retrieve the gold, the Roman commander ordered that the temple be dismantled stone by stone. The destruction was so complete that today they have true difficulty learning exactly where the foundation of the temple was.

iii. "Josephus says the stones were white and strong; fifty feet long, twenty-four broad, and sixteen thick. Antiq. b. 15. c. xi." (Clarke)

e. **That shall not be thrown down:** This prophecy was fulfilled literally. There was a real temple, and it was really destroyed. The literal fulfillment of this prophecy establishes the tone for the rest of the prophecies in the chapter.[3]

Jesus also prophesied, "And they will fall by the edge of the sword, and be led away captive into all nations" (Luke 21:24).

Live Science, a respected secular source, said of ancient Israel,

In A.D. 66, tensions between the region's Jewish inhabitants and Roman rulers came to a head. A rebellion started and culminated in A.D. 70 in the siege of Jerusalem and the destruction of the second temple...

Further rebellions occurred over the decades. The final rebellion was crushed in A.D. 136. The ancient writer Cassius Dio (lived ca. A.D. 155–235) wrote that this last rebellion led to the desolation of the Jewish population. He claimed that Roman forces killed about 580,000 Jewish men.

"Five hundred and eighty thousand men were slain in the various raids and battles, and the number of those that perished by famine, disease and fire was past finding out... thus nearly the whole of Judaea was made desolate," Dio wrote... Archaeologists are still finding treasure hoards buried by people who lived during the rebellion.

In the millennia afterward, the Jewish diaspora spread throughout the world. It wasn't until the establishment of the modern state of Israel in 1948 that the Jewish people had a homeland again.[4]

For the next two thousand years, the Jews were without a homeland. They were expected to have disappeared as did the other cultures of the ancient Near East, yet they amazingly retained their identity as a people.

Reborn in a Day

Then in 1948 another specific Old Testament prophecy found fulfillment in our times when Israel was miraculously reborn in a day:

Isaiah asked, "Who has ever seen things like this? Can a country be born in a day or a nation be brought forth in a moment?" (Isaiah 66:8). After nearly two millennia and a succession of foreign rulers, on May 14, 1948, David Ben Gurion declared the restoration of the Jewish State, Israel.[5]

In 1948 the State of Israel became a nation, and the Jewish people flooded back to the land. Again, they didn't have a homeland and should have ceased to be a recognizable people group.

In speaking of this, Israel's Ministry of Foreign Affairs stated,

The birthplace of the Jewish people is the Land of Israel (Eretz Yisrael). There, a significant part of the nation's long history was enacted, of which the first thousand years are recorded in the Bible; there, its cultural, religious, and national identity was formed; and there, its physical presence has been maintained through the centuries, even after the majority was forced into exile. During the many years of dispersion, the Jewish people never severed nor forgot its bond with the

Land. With the establishment of the State of Israel in 1948, Jewish independence, lost 2,000 years earlier, was renewed.[6]

Five hundred years before Jesus was born, God said that He would scatter the Jews among the nations, and that they would return to their land:

> "I will sow them among the peoples,
> And they shall remember Me in far countries;
> They shall live, together with their children,
> And they shall return." (Zechariah 10:9)

Then, in 1967, another prophecy was fulfilled when the Jews possessed Jerusalem once again. Remember, in Luke 21:24, Jesus foretold, "And Jerusalem will be trampled by Gentiles until the times of the Gentiles are fulfilled." Right up until 1967, Jerusalem was under Gentile control.

Encyclopaedia Britannica explains how Israel reacquired its capital city:

> Arab and Israeli forces clashed for the third time June 5–10, 1967, in what came to be called the Six-Day War (or June War). In early 1967 Syria intensified its bombardment of Israeli villages from positions in the Golan Heights. When the Israeli Air Force shot down six Syrian MiG fighter jets in reprisal, Nasser mobilized his forces near the Sinai border, dismissing the UN force there, and he again sought to blockade Elat. In May

1967 Egypt signed a mutual defense pact with Jordan.

Israel answered this apparent Arab rush to war by staging a sudden air assault, destroying Egypt's air force on the ground. The Israeli victory on the ground was also overwhelming. Israeli units drove back Syrian forces from the Golan Heights, took control of the Gaza Strip and the Sinai Peninsula from Egypt, and drove Jordanian forces from the West Bank. Importantly, the Israelis were left in sole control of Jerusalem.[7]

Another article from June 2020 gives further details:

JERUSALEM, Israel — Fifty-three years ago, Israeli soldiers captured the Old City of Jerusalem.

On June 7, 1967, the 55th Paratrooper Brigade of Commander Mordechai (Motta) Gur broke through Jordanian defenses. What happened next resonated throughout the world and electrified the Jewish people.

Commander Gur broke the radio silence and said, "the Temple Mount is in our hands."

It marked the first time the Jewish people controlled Judaism's holiest site in more than 2,000 years.

"Within six days, we returned to the biblical land of Israel, all the mountains of Judea, Samaria, the Golan Heights. We returned to the Old City of Jerusalem," Rabbi Yehudah Glick told CBN News.

"It was liberated and reunited and here we are 53 years later, a new government, Jerusalem is united. It's fabulous, it's the Word of God coming out of the book, materializing and becoming a reality in our time in front of our eyes."

Israel's victory in the Six-Day war stunned the world and became a turning point for Jewish immigration back to their land.

"Throughout the Old Testament God says that he is going to draw the Jewish people back to the land. But what is interesting is at that moment, when Mordechai Gur, the Israeli general said on the radio, 'the Temple Mount is in our hands.' When that was broadcast, not just through Israel but worldwide, it electrified Jewish communities all over the planet. The level of Aliyah, Jews leaving their exile countries and coming back to the land of their forefathers skyrocketed in the years ahead," explained author *New York Times* best-selling author Joel Rosenberg.

Yet more than 50 years since the battle for Jerusalem, Rosenberg says Israel and its capital remain on the front lines.

"Jerusalem is the epicenter," he told CBN News. "You know for 4,000 years people have wanted this city and they have fought hard to get it. And so, the fact that Israel controls it today is biblical, it's prophetic but it's also complicated, and we need to be praying for the peace of Jerusalem and praying for Israel to be secure."[8]

The Bible also prophesied that Israel would once again be restored as a fertile land and the desert would bloom:

> The prophet Isaiah foretold a time when "the desert and the parched land will be glad; the wilderness will rejoice and blossom" (Isaiah 35:1). In her short time of existence as a modern State, Israel is known for its abundant flowers and produce. Desert lands have become fertile farms.[9]

We will look at another fascinating prophecy about Jerusalem in the next chapter.

CHAPTER THREE

A BURDEN TO THE NATIONS

THE NATION OF ISRAEL began two thousand years before Christ, with Jacob and his twelve sons. Contemporary nations such as Elam, Chaldea, the Hittite empire, and others are long gone, but Israel still exists, and not in obscurity. It has become the forefront of international concern.

Consider the specific wording used in Scripture:

> "And in that day will I make Jerusalem a burdensome stone for all people: all that burden themselves with it shall be cut in pieces, though all the people of the earth be gathered together against it." (Zechariah 12:3, KJV)

The Scriptures speak of a time when the city of Jerusalem would be a massive problem for everyone—a burdensome stone for all people. The modern maxim would be that the city of Jerusalem has become *a pain in the neck* for the nations of the world.

For many years the Jewish people had no true home. As prophecy had said thousands of years earlier, they would "become an astonishment, a proverb, and a byword among all nations where the LORD will drive you" (Deuteronomy 28:37).

They are now back in their own nation, and despite the fact that the surrounding Muslim nations passionately want to annihilate Israel, the Jewish people have been insistent that they hold their present boundaries.

But the great treasure of Jerusalem—which since the days of Jesus had been in the hands of the Romans, the Syrians, the Arabs, Crusaders, Egyptians, Persians, and Turks—became theirs again in 1967. They finally gained control of the city.

The United Nations

On December 23, 2016, the United Nations Security Council had passed a resolution to divide Jerusalem. Fourteen nations (China, France, Russia, United Kingdom, Angola, Egypt, Japan, Malaysia, New Zealand, Senegal, Spain, Ukraine, Uruguay, and Venezuela) voted for the resolution, with the US abstaining.

Not one of those voting nations were forced to take on this task and vote to divide the Holy City; they did so voluntarily. They stepped forward in unison to try to lift the "burdensome stone." But it will not move. The annoying pain in the neck remains, and many believe it will stay until the coming battle of Armageddon. Dr. Herbert Hillel Goldberg writes:

> "With regard to the war preparations by Muslim states to the north of Israel, and the ever-deeper involvement of Russia, there is a distinct development towards the prophesied attack of Gog of Magog against Israel (Ezek. 38 and 39)—and the dispute revolves around Jerusalem. Should we fear? God said: "I will punish him with pestilence and with blood; torrential rain and great hailstones, fire and brimstone will I rain upon him and upon his bands, and upon the many peoples that are with him" (38:22).

It also states: "In that day the LORD shall defend the inhabitants of Jerusalem . . . And it shall come to pass on that day, that I will seek to destroy all the nations that come against Jerusalem" (Zech. 12:8-9).[10]

Author Steven M. Collins explains what makes Israel a "burdensome stone":

Why is Jerusalem such an insoluble problem for the nations of the world? It would be no problem at all except for the fact that God fulfilled his prophecy in Zephaniah 2:1–10 that the house of Judah (the Jews) would again have a homeland in the old Promised Land *just prior* to "the Day of the Lord's anger." That prophecy was fulfilled in 1948 when the new Jewish nation came into existence in a territory that included the coastal Mediterranean Sea region and the city of Ashkelon, just as Zephaniah 2:7 foretold.

Interestingly, the prophecy in Zephaniah 2 about the founding of the state of Israel in the latter days *does not* include a reference to the city of Jerusalem; however, the prophecies in Zechariah 12 and 14 about the very end of the age do mention Judah and Jerusalem together as if they were synonymously linked. This indicates that the Jews would not have full control over the city of Jerusalem at the beginning of their national history, but that they would have a clear possession of the city at the end of the age (which is exactly

how history has un-
folded from 1948
until today).

The city of
Jerusalem would
not be a "burden-
some stone" for
the nations of the
world unless the
Jews had posses-
sion of the city
and especially if they make it their capital
city. While the Jews have regarded Jerusalem
as their true capital city since the Israeli
nation was founded, other nations have not
recognized that claim.[11]

National Consequences

Look at this prophecy again, and note the promised
repercussions for those nations that turn against
Israel:

> Behold, I will make Jerusalem a cup of trem-
> bling unto all the people round about, when
> they shall be in the siege both against Judah
> and against Jerusalem. And in that day will I
> make Jerusalem a burdensome stone for all
> people: all that burden themselves with it
> shall be cut in pieces, though all the people
> of the earth be gathered together against it.
> (Zechariah 12:2,3, KJV)

Popular Bible commentator J. Vernon McGee said of these verses:

> Now let me call your attention to something that is exceedingly strange. Although the fulfillment of this prophecy will not be until the end times, we have noted something that has been going on for years. Every nation in the history of the world that has attempted to control Jerusalem has been destroyed or has gone into decline. The day that Great Britain took the sphere of influence over the land of Israel and began to control Jerusalem—from that day to this—we have seen the decline of Great Britain from the first-rate nation of the world to the third-rate nation it is today.
>
> Personally, I do not think this is an accident. God said through Zechariah that He would "make Jerusalem a burdensome stone for all people," and I think that God wants us to keep our hands off that nation. I hope my nation will do that, by the way. A great many people think we ought to intrude in the affairs of Israel on one side or the other, but Israel is a sensitive spot on this earth as far as God is concerned.[12]

Peace and Safety Promised

Another sign of the times preceding "the day of the Lord" is that the world would believe it has entered a time of peace and safety:

But concerning the times and the seasons, brethren, you have no need that I should write to you. For you yourselves know perfectly that the day of the Lord so comes as a thief in the night. For when they say, "Peace and safety!" then sudden destruction comes upon them, as labor pains upon a pregnant woman. And they shall not escape. But you, brethren, are not in darkness, so that this Day should overtake you as a thief. (1 Thessalonians 5:1–5)

Any genuine and lasting peace negotiations between Arabs and Jews can't really be appreciated without a little history as to how complicated the conflict has been.

Someone once said:

"Look, this isn't *rocket science!*" We hear the phrase from teachers when they want their students to know when an issue isn't that complex. But there's a problem with this phrase: it implies that rocket science represents the ceiling of human intelligence, and in using it we leave our rocket scientist professors without a complex problem of their own to which they can refer. So here's a phrase that might be helpful: "Look, this isn't the *Israeli-Palestinian conflict!*"[13]

The Jewish people have had a rocky history. They had their homeland under King David and

King Solomon, but then they were conquered by the Syrians, taken as slaves by the Babylonians, and eventually scattered throughout the world in AD 70.

As Islam began to grow in the seventh century, Muslims controlled the Middle East region and built mosques on Jewish holy sites. However, Arabs and Jews were able to live side-by-side in the Ottoman Empire. After the First World War ended in 1918, the Empire collapsed and both Jews and Arabs wanted to form their own states. The hope was that the Arabs who lived in modern-day Palestine, Syria, Lebanon, Iraq, and Saudi Arabia would live in harmony with the Jews.

When the British took control of Palestine, they attempted to give the Jews a homeland through the Balfour Declaration, but the Arabs didn't want to give up their land. Britain didn't know how to fix this problem and eventually gave the territory to the United Nations, which decided to divide Palestine into a Jewish state and an Arab state.

That seemed like an amicable resolution. But it was not to be. When the Jews declared their independence in 1948, the Arabs in Palestine joined forces with the Arabs from the surrounding nations to attack Israel.

Israel was victorious in that conflict, securing their independence and driving out 700,000 Palestinians. Since then Arabs have claimed that the refugees and their children have the right to return to Palestine.

Then in 1967, the Arab nations secured troops around Israel and threatened to annihilate it. However, in a preemptive strike, Israel defeated its enemies in a mere six days (the "Six Day War"). They began building settlements in the West Bank area, evicting its Arab occupants. Since that time there has been continual conflict in the West Bank. But that's only one problem. There is also continual conflict as to who has ownership of sites considered holy to both Jews and Muslims.

However, in August 2020, there came the "Abrahamic" peace accord:

> In forging the first Arab-Israeli peace deal since 1994, President Donald Trump paid homage to a patriarch.
>
> He named the historic normalization the "Abraham Accord."
>
> The familiar Bible character "is referred to as 'Abraham' in the Christian faith, 'Ibrahim' in the Muslim faith, and 'Avraham' in the Jewish faith," explained David Friedman, US ambassador to Israel.
>
> "And no person better symbolizes the potential for unity, among all these three great faiths."
>
> In signing the accord, the United Arab Emirates (UAE) joined Egypt and Jordan as the only Arab nations to make peace with Israel. Telephone lines are already being connected between the Gulf nation and the

Jewish state, with preparations underway to exchange embassies.

It may open a new era. Fellow Gulf nations Bahrain and Oman signaled their support, while Saudi Arabia did not oppose it.

"This is a once-in-a-generation diplomatic achievement, but I predict it will be the first, not the last," said Johnnie Moore, an evangelical leader engaged in behind-the-scenes advocacy. He and bestselling novelist Joel Rosenberg led an evangelical delegation to the UAE in October 2018 (as well as two delegations to Saudi Arabia), and Moore has personally visited three more times.

"The Abraham Accord," he said, "will prove to be the moment when the grievances of the past no longer overpowered the promises of the future in the Middle East."[14]

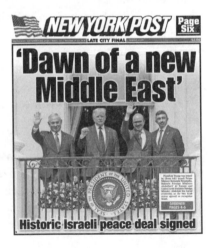

In August 2020, the BBC reported "Trump announces 'peace deal' between Bahrain and Israel":

Israel and the Gulf state of Bahrain have reached a landmark deal to fully normalize their relations, US President Donald Trump has announced.

"The second Arab country to make peace with Israel in 30 days," he tweeted.

For decades, most Arab states have boycotted Israel, insisting they would only establish ties after the Palestinian dispute was settled.

But last month the United Arab Emirates (UAE) agreed to normalise its relationship with Israel.

There had been much speculation that Bahrain might follow suit.

Mr Trump, who presented his Middle East peace plan in January aimed at resolving the Israel-Palestinian conflict, helped broker both accords.

Bahrain is only the fourth Arab country in the Middle East—after the UAE, Egypt and Jordan—to recognize Israel since its founding in 1948.[15]

The *New York Times* said of this giant leap:

The announcement that Bahrain would establish full diplomatic relations with Israel leaves open the possibility that more Arab states will follow... Other Arab countries are likely to follow Bahrain and the United Arab

Emirates in recognizing Israel, with Sudan and Oman potential candidates, according to some analysts. But Bahrain's decision is tantalizing because of its close ties and dependence on its much larger neighbor, Saudi Arabia.[16]

Two years earlier, President Trump moved the US Embassy to Jerusalem, acknowledging the city as the capital of Israel. At that time the BBC reported:

The Reverend Johnnie Moore agrees that some evangelicals hold premillennial, or dispensationalist, beliefs. But he thinks it's a "very, very small group", whose influence is exaggerated.

"I've seen all the stories," he says. "'Evangelicals want Armageddon' or 'Evangelicals want the Rapture'.

"I think that is Exhibit A of people on the outside coming to conclusions about what evangelicals actually think."

Evangelicals did discuss Jerusalem in the White House. But the discussions, says Mr Moore, were political—not theological.

"The leaders know what they're talking about from experience," he says.

"They follow politics in the region, they know the public figures, they read the papers, they have informed foreign policy views.

"This was geo-political opinion, more than theology."

The message is echoed by David Brog, executive director of Christians United for Israel.

"There is a widespread myth that Christians support Israel to speed the End Times," he says. "That's simply not true.

"Anyone who understands the theology / eschatology of pro-Israel Christians knows they believe they are powerless to change the date of End Times.

"If they are powerless to speed this day, their support for Israel must be driven by other motives.

"In the case of Jerusalem, we support President Trump's decision because it is an act of historic justice—and an overdue recognition of modern reality."[17]

Way back on June 3, 1855, influential preacher Charles Spurgeon said of the restoration of the Jews to their homeland:

I think we do not attach sufficient importance to the restoration of the Jews. We do not think enough about it. But certainly, if there is anything promised in the Bible it is this. I imagine that you cannot read the Bible without seeing clearly that there is to be an actual restoration of the Children of Israel... For when the Jews are restored, the fullness of the Gentiles shall be gathered in; and as soon as they return, then Jesus will come upon

Mount Zion with his ancients gloriously, and the halcyon days of the millennium shall then dawn; we shall then know every man to be a brother and a friend; Christ shall rule with universal sway.[18]

When the Prince of Preachers mentioned Jesus coming "with his ancients," he was referring to the glorious Second Coming of Jesus:

Now Enoch, the seventh from Adam, prophesied about these men also, saying, "Behold, the Lord comes with ten thousands of His saints, to execute judgment on all, to convict all who are ungodly among them of all their ungodly deeds which they have committed in an ungodly way, and of all the harsh things which ungodly sinners have spoken against Him." (Jude 14,15)

After Spurgeon spoke of the restoration, it would be another ninety-three years before the words of Jesus would be fulfilled and the nation of Israel would be returned to their homeland.

Here is the big question: *Are these actually biblical prophecies being fulfilled in our time?* Spurgeon looked forward to a foggy future. We have the privilege of looking back to a clear past, and can therefore have more confidence that we are unique and privileged witnesses to prophetic dominoes.

CHAPTER FOUR

JOSH DROPS A BOMBSHELL

> But know this, that in
> the last days perilous
> times will come: For
> men will be lovers of
> themselves, lovers of
> money, boasters, proud,
> ~~disobedient~~

I WAS SURPRISED that Josh had continued listening to me as I spoke about the Bible. I suspected that he would disagree, mainly because he was delving into the dark world of tarot cards. But he was politely listening, so I continued to speak:

RAY: So, if you want a prediction of what tomorrow is about, just read the Bible. Have you ever read the Bible?

JOSH: Yeah.

RAY: Do you know what its message is?

JOSH: No.

RAY: Well, in the Old Testament, God promised to destroy death. The New Testament tells us how He did it. Do you think there's an afterlife?

JOSH: Yes!

RAY: Why are you so adamant? You are very quick to say yes.

JOSH: It's just what I believe.

RAY: Is it based on anything?

JOSH: I would have to think about it a lot more.

RAY: Is it based on hope? You just love life and would hate death to be the end?

JOSH: I think I'm a very optimistic person, so you could say that.

RAY: You're afraid of death?

JOSH: Not particularly.

RAY: I think everybody is. People who say "not particularly" are either proud and they don't want people to know they're vulnerable, or they haven't thought about it very deeply. But if you think about it, your life is so precious to you. If you've got a contagious disease that led to death, you'd be saying, "Oh God, I don't want to die! I don't want to die. I love life. I love the blue sky and love and laughter and music and friends and family and food, and all these things that surround us." Do you believe God exists?

JOSH: No.

RAY: You're an atheist?

JOSH: Yes, I am.

RAY: What led you to atheism?

JOSH: I'm queer.

Rampant Immorality

I didn't expect that answer. Most prefer to use a softer word to describe their sexuality. I didn't say anything to Josh at that time because I cared about him and wanted him to keep listening. However, another sign of the end of the age is that people would be proud and blasphemous, lovers of themselves, and lovers of pleasure (see 2 Timothy 3:1–5). It seems that the entire world is given to rampant and boundless sexual sin—whether it is fornication, adultery, pornography, or homosexuality. More and more people are forsaking marriage in favor of shacking up.

> Among those ages 18–24, cohabitation is now more prevalent than living with a spouse: 9 percent live with an unmarried partner in 2018, compared to 7 percent who live with a spouse. In 2018, 15 percent of young adults ages 25–34 live with an unmarried partner… Fifty years ago, in 1968, living with an unmarried partner was rare. Only 0.1 percent of 18- to 24-year-olds and 0.2 percent of 25- to 34-year-olds lived with an unmarried partner, according to the Current Population Survey.[19]

Is marriage becoming obsolete? Statistics suggest it's not faring well. In 1960, 72 percent of Americans were married; that fell to 51 percent in 2011. What's more, popular media and some research estimates suggest that nearly half of people in long-term relationships "get some on the side." Finally, to put the icing on the (any kind but wedding) cake, Gallup reports that the percentage of people who think "polygamy" is not morally objectionable increased from 7 to 16 percent between 2001 and 2015.[20]

A friend appeared on CNN's *Piers Morgan Live* back in 2012 and shared his convictions on gay marriage. When asked, he simply said, "I think that it's unnatural. I think that it's detrimental and ultimately destructive to so many of the foundations of civilization." He then added, "One man, one woman for life 'till death do you part'. . . So do I support the idea of gay marriage? No, I don't."

He certainly didn't expect the vicious backlash that came against him.

Piers Morgan defended his right to speak out, however "antiquated" his beliefs. In an interview, Morgan called him "pretty brave" for voicing his opinion. "I felt that he was honest to what he believed, and I don't think he was expecting the furor that it created," Morgan said.

The gay-rights group GLAAD, meanwhile, slammed his remarks as "dated." "[He] is out of step with a growing majority of Americans, particularly people of faith who believe that their gay and lesbian brothers and sisters should be loved and accepted based on their character and not condemned because of their sexual orientation," the organization said in a statement.

Every Christian should love gay and lesbian people. We should also love adulterers and fornicators, liars and thieves. But because we love them, we *must* tell them the truth—that if they refuse to repent, they will not enter the Kingdom of God:

> Do you not know that the unrighteous will not inherit the kingdom of God? Do not be deceived. Neither fornicators, nor idolaters, nor adulterers, nor homosexuals, nor sodomites, nor thieves, nor covetous, nor drunkards, nor revilers, nor extortioners will inherit the kingdom of God. (1 Corinthians 6:9,10)

And my faithful friend loved homosexuals enough to tell them the truth, outdated though many may believe it is. God is never outdated. He doesn't change. Sin, no matter how celebrated it may become, is *never* acceptable to Him.

In describing an ancient Roman civilization that gave itself to homosexuality, Scripture addresses how they first rejected God:

> For since the creation of the world His invisible attributes are clearly seen, being understood by the things that are made, even His eternal power and Godhead, so that they are without excuse, because, although they knew God, they did not glorify Him as God, nor were thankful, but became futile in their thoughts, and their foolish hearts were darkened. Professing to be wise, they became fools, and changed the glory of the incorruptible God into an image made like corruptible man—and birds and four-footed animals and creeping things. (Romans 1:20–23)

When human beings give themselves to *any* sexual sin, they often either deny the existence of God, or more commonly, reshape His character to accommodate their sins—something the Bible calls "idolatry."

It normally sounds like this: "I believe in God, but my god doesn't condemn people to everlasting punishment because they were born a particular way." Or, "My god is a god of love and mercy. He loves and forgives *everybody*." When we make up our own image of God, we violate the First and the Second of the Ten Commandments:

> You shall have no other gods before Me.

> You shall not make for yourself a carved image... (Exodus 20:3,4)

This was the sin of this Roman civilization, with the expected slide into immorality:

> Therefore God also gave them up to uncleanness, in the lusts of their hearts, to dishonor their bodies among themselves, who exchanged the truth of God for the lie, and worshiped and served the creature rather than the Creator, who is blessed forever. Amen.
>
> For this reason God gave them up to vile passions. For even their women exchanged the natural use for what is against nature. Likewise also the men, leaving the natural use of the woman, burned in their lust for one another, men with men committing what is shameful, and receiving in themselves the penalty of their error which was due. (Romans 1:24–27)

Often homosexuals try to justify their sin by saying that there's nothing wrong with "loving" someone. But the Scriptures speak of homosexuality as "against nature" and a "vile passion." A commentary notes:

> The descent into evolutionary paganism is always soon followed by gross immorality, specifically including sexual perversion, such as described in Romans 1:26–29. Ancient Sodom was so notorious for homosexuality that its practice has long been known as sod-

omy (see Genesis 13:13; 19:4–9). The practice became so widespread in ancient Greece that it was considered normal and even desirable. Other examples are abundant and, of course, it is quickly becoming accepted—even encouraged—here in America. Not surprisingly, this was preceded by widespread return to evolutionism in science and education.[21]

Then Scripture predicts that those who give themselves to idolatry or atheism will eventually descend into a multitude of sins:

> And even as they did not like to retain God in their knowledge, God gave them over to a debased mind, to do those things which are not fitting; being filled with all unrighteousness, sexual immorality, wickedness, covetousness, maliciousness; full of envy, murder, strife, deceit, evil-mindedness; they are whisperers, backbiters, haters of God, violent, proud, boasters, inventors of evil things, disobedient to parents, undiscerning, untrustworthy, unloving, unforgiving, unmerciful; who, knowing the righteous judgment of God, that those who practice such things are deserving of death, not only do the same but also approve of those who practice them. (Romans 1:28–32)

Atheism and Homosexuality

RAY: Well, *that* [being homosexual] doesn't make you an atheist.

JOSH: Well, it led me to it.

RAY: Why?

JOSH: Because I'm queer, and queer people have been persecuted like a lot of other people. When I was growing up and I was in high school reading about the Holocaust (because that's what our curriculum teaches us in grade school), I thought about how horrible some of these things were and then I thought about the concept of Hell—which is an afterlife concept and something I choose not to believe in sometimes. I just thought about how some entity so powerful [is] supposed to love the people that they created, and you see all the tragedies and terrible crises that happen on earth throughout history—and even the things that we're living through right now—I could not fathom an entity letting all those things happen.

RAY: You brought up the Holocaust. I'm Jewish. I wrote a book called *Hitler, God, and the Bible*, and as I went into writing the book, as I researched it, in my subconscious I was thinking, "How could God ever create Hell?" After studying the Holocaust and seeing what Hitler did to the Jews and homosexuals and gypsies and blacks (horror beyond words that had me in tears), I came out of that saying, "How could God *not* create Hell?" There *must* be punishment for evil if God is just and good and holy. There must be retribution or God is wicked and evil—because any judge who turns a blind eye to such wickedness and says, "I don't care," is evil by nature.

Okay, Josh, let me change the dynamic a little if you don't mind. We've addressed your intellect. I'd like to address your conscience; are you okay with that?

JOSH: Of course.

RAY: Do you think you're a good person?

JOSH: I think so.

RAY: How many lies have you told in your life?

JOSH: A lot.

RAY: What do you call someone who tells lies?

JOSH: You call him a liar; that's something really basic.

RAY: Have you ever stolen something in your whole life, even if it's small, irrespective of its value?

JOSH: I plead the fifth on that one.

[To "plead the fifth" means to refuse to answer a question, especially in a criminal trial, on the grounds that you might incriminate yourself.]

RAY: Have you ever used God's name in vain?

JOSH: I will plead the fifth on that one too.

RAY: Jesus said, if you look with lust you commit adultery in your heart. Have you ever looked with lust?

JOSH: I have no problem saying that I have been lusty in my life.

RAY: The reason we die is because we've sinned against God. The Bible says, "The *wages* of sin is death" [see Romans 6:23]. In other words, sin is so serious to God that He is paying you in death for your sins. It's like a judge who has a criminal in front of him who has raped three girls and then slit their throats. The judge says, "You've *earned* the death sentence. This is your *wages*; this is what's due to you." He says, "You've *earned* your punishment."

And God says our sin is so serious, He has given us the death sen-  tence. We're waiting around to die because we're on death row—because God said that the soul who sins shall die. The proof that God is serious about sin will be our death. And then after death, the Bible says damnation if you die in your sins. This is because God's going to judge you, not from man's perspective—we all think we're good—but from His perspective, which is one of absolute moral perfection, what the Bible calls "holiness."

* * *

In the next chapter, we will address the question, "Does the God of love and mercy send plagues upon humanity?" Then we will continue the conversation with Josh and hear what else the God of mercy offers to us all.

CHAPTER FIVE

DOES GOD SEND PLAGUES?

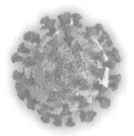

IF YOU WANT TO see the wrath of an unbelieving world, just hint that God sent the COVID-19 pandemic as a judgment for our sinful ways.

It may be offensive to those whose image of God is one of a benevolent father figure, but those who know their Bibles will also know that God *often* sent plagues upon sinful and unrepentant nations. He did this to shake them (see Amos 9:9, Haggai 2:7; Hebrews 12:26). It is His purpose that when our knees go weak, we drop to them and seek the divine will.

In the book of Exodus, God warned Egypt's leaders of what would happen if they refused to humble themselves and obey Him:

> Then the LORD said to Moses, "Go in to Pharaoh and tell him, 'Thus says the LORD

God of the Hebrews: "Let My people go, that
they may serve Me. For if you refuse to let
them go, and still hold them, behold, the
hand of the LORD will be on your cattle in
the field, on the horses, on the donkeys, on
the camels, on the oxen, and on the sheep—*a
very severe pestilence*."" (Exodus 9:1–3)

So the LORD sent a plague upon Israel from
the morning till the appointed time. From
Dan to Beersheba seventy thousand men of
the people died. (2 Samuel 24:15)

Jesus also called these plagues "pestilences," and
He indicated they would be among the signs of the
end times. According to the *Merriam-Webster* dic-
tionary, *pestilence* is "a contagious or infectious epi-
demic disease that is virulent and devastating."

Here are Jesus' prophetic words from Matthew's
Gospel:

Now as He sat on the Mount of Olives, the
disciples came to Him privately, saying, "Tell
us, when will these things be? And what will
be the sign of Your coming, and of the end of
the age?"

And Jesus answered and said to them:
"Take heed that no one deceives you. For
many will come in My name, saying, 'I am
the Christ,' and will deceive many. And you
will hear of wars and rumors of wars. See
that you are not troubled; for all these things
must come to pass, but the end is not yet. For

nation will rise against nation, and kingdom against kingdom. And there will be famines, *pestilences*, and earthquakes in various places. All these are the beginning of sorrows." (Matthew 24:3–8)

Jesus had just spoken of the destruction of Jerusalem. Then the disciples asked Him two questions: "Tell us, when will these things be?" First, they wanted to know details about the judgment of Jerusalem. Then came the second question: "And what will be the sign of Your coming, and of the end of the age?"

They wanted to know the specific "sign" of the Second Coming, to which He responded that they should be aware of 1) coming deception, 2) wars, 3) nation rising against nation, 4) famines, 5) pestilences, and 6) earthquakes.

The Gospel of Luke gives more details of the same discourse:

Then He said to them, "Nation will rise against nation, and kingdom against kingdom. And there will be great earthquakes in various places, and famines and pestilences; and there will be fearful sights and great signs from heaven. But before all these things, they will lay their hands on you and persecute you, delivering you up to the synagogues and prisons. You will be brought before kings and rulers for My name's sake." (Luke 21:10–12)

He reaffirmed that there would be pestilences, adding there would also be fearful sights, signs from Heaven, and persecution for those who trust in Him.

All these things—deception, wars, nation rising against nation, famines, pestilences, and earthquakes—have been around for millennia. But the Jews being back in Jerusalem has not.

The Timelines

There are at least two interpretations of the timelines of these prophecies. Some believe that these signs became evident soon after He predicted them, with the destruction of the temple in Jerusalem (AD 70). Others believe that they have been more evident in recent years, showing us that the Second Coming will soon take place.

Whether you come to the conclusion that AD 70 was the era when these things came to pass, or you believe that they are yet to be fulfilled, the most important point is that Jesus spoke the future before it came into being. *That is evidence of His divinity.* That's why we should obey the gospel. It's not that I have some sort of fascination for the future, but I'm concerned for *your* future. I want to see you in Heaven, and not end up in Hell. And this was my earnest goal with Josh, because I loved him:

RAY: Now tell me, what did God do for guilty sinners so we wouldn't have to go to Hell? Do you know?

JOSH: Go for it, tell me.

RAY: Well, the Ten Commandments are called the moral Law. You and I broke the Law, Jesus came and paid the fine—that's what happened on the cross.

Do you know what His last words were just before He died? There were three words. He said, "It is finished." That's a weird thing to say when you're dying. Some people try to say something profound or philosophical, or just "Arghhhh." But He said, "It is finished." In other words, "The debt has been paid."

[In New Testament times, the Greek word *tetelestai* (literally "It is finished") was also written on business documents and receipts to indicate that a bill was paid in full. Jesus' audience very clearly understood His meaning—that He died to pay their sin debt in full.]

RAY: We broke the Law; He paid the fine. Josh, if you're in court and someone pays your fine, the judge can let you go even though you're guilty. He can say, "Joshua, there's a stack of speeding fines here; this is deadly serious, but someone's paid them—you're

free to go." And he can do that which is legal and right and just.

You and I are guilty before God; we've violated His Law. We can plead the fifth if we want, but all of us are guilty. And if you hate someone, the Bible says you're a murderer in your heart as far as God is concerned—that's how high His standard is. We're under His wrath, under the death sentence, heading for Hell, but God paid the fine in Christ so that justice could be done and mercy could be extended.

Jesus Christ died on the cross. That means God can freely let you live forever, not because you're good, but because *He's* good and kind and rich in mercy. Then Jesus rose from the dead and defeated death.

I notice on your book there you've got a skull. [I aimed the camera at an occult book by the tarot cards.]

It's usually depicting death. Death is called "The Grim Reaper." Jesus took the sickle out of the hand of the Grim Reaper. Death lost its sting when Jesus rose from the dead, and now God offers you everlasting life as a free gift, if you'll simply repent of all sin. That means lying, stealing, lust, homosexuality, adultery, fornication—whatever you know the Bible says.

JOSH: Is homosexuality a sin? Is that where we're going with this?

RAY: I have to mention it to you to be faithful, because I love you. I care about you—and I'm not going to lie to you for fear of offending you. The Bible makes it very clear in the book of Corinthians.

JOSH: Feel free to be honest here. I mean, if that's your belief that it's a sin, please; I think that that's really important to lay out on the table.

RAY: Homosexuals say, "I was *born* with the desires. I had no choice." Well, I was *born* with a desire to commit adultery when I looked at the lady next door from when I was a little kid. She was gorgeous. I'd love to go to bed with her, but it doesn't make it right. "Do not be deceived. Neither thieves, liars, fornicators, adulterers, homosexuals will inherit the kingdom of God." So anyway, back to what I was saying. If you will repent of all sin (that which you know was offensive to God), God says He'll not only forgive you...

JOSH: Straight people aren't offensive to God?

RAY: They are absolutely under the death sentence. If I've looked with lust, as far as God is concerned, I've committed adultery in my heart. Jesus said that in the Sermon on the Mount [see Matthew 5:27,28]. I'm a liar, and a thief, and a fornicator; I've committed all those sins. I'm as guilty as the rest. So, homosexuality isn't being singled out as a particular sin— it's just in the list of sins.

JOSH: We're not talking about the same thing. When you talk about homosexuality, you're talking about that, compared to something else that isn't an actual "relationship." You know, simple fornication is not a relationship, adultery is not a relationship. These are all things that stand alone on their own as sins, right? You're not comparing a queer relationship to a straight relationship the right way.

RAY: All of us have sinned; we all have God's wrath abiding upon us. We are under His death sentence, but God offers everlasting life to the whole of humanity: adulterers, fornicators, homosexuals, liars, thieves…If you'll simply repent of *all* sin and trust in Jesus for your salvation, God promises more than to commute your death sentence.

[You may have noticed I kept emphasizing to Josh that he must repent of all sin to be saved. This is because there are some who say that repentance is not necessary to enter Heaven—that we need only "believe." This is a great error, because those who don't repent will perish (see Luke 13:1–4). Puritan preacher and author Thomas Watson (1620–1686) said,

> The two great graces essential to a saint in this life are faith and repentance. These are the two wings by which he flies to heaven. Faith and repentance preserve the spiritual life as heat and radical moisture do the natural. The grace which I am going to discuss is repentance.
>
> Chrysostom thought it the fittest subject for him to preach upon before the Emperor Arcadius. Augustine caused the penitential psalms to be written before him as he lay upon his bed, and he often perused them with tears. Repentance is never out of season; it is of as frequent use as the artificer's tool or the soldier's weapon. If I am not mistaken, practical points are more needful in this age than controversial and polemical.
>
> I had thought to have smothered these meditations in my desk, but, conceiving them to be of great concern at this juncture of time, I have rescinded my first resolution and have exposed them to a critical view.
>
> Repentance is purgative; fear not the working of this pill. Smite your soul, said Chrysostom, smite it; it will escape death by that stroke. How happy it would be if we were more deeply affected with sin, and our eyes did swim in their orb. We may clearly see the Spirit of God moving in the waters of repen-

tance, which though troubled, are yet pure. Moist tears dry up sin and quench the wrath of God. Repentance is the cherisher of piety, the procurer of mercy. The more regret and trouble of spirit we have first at our conversion, the less we shall feel afterwards.[22]]

RAY: Do you know the difference between a commutation and a pardon?

JOSH: Yes.

RAY: Well, God doesn't just *commute* your sins, He *pardons* them completely—as though you never sinned. He clothes you in righteousness, so that when you stand before Him on Judgment Day, He can legally let you live forever, because Jesus died on the cross.

JOSH: Living forever would be such a burden, though.

RAY: Well, it won't be in that state. We live in a *fallen* state—with futility, and pain, and suffering, and loneliness, and fear. God says He's going to take all that away, no more tears, pain, suffering, and death. God's Kingdom is coming to this earth, and God's will will be done on this earth as it is in Heaven.

This has been a very stimulating conversation; I've really enjoyed it, and I want to thank you so much for listening to me and being so reasonable. I want you to realize that I don't condemn you as a homosexual, I love you as a homosexual. I care about you.

Are you going to think about what we talked about today? I mean the gospel I shared with you, that God offers everlasting life as a free gift to all...

JOSH: Absolutely not, because I don't believe in Him.

RAY: As I said, I love you and the thought of you ending up in Hell breaks my heart; it really does. I don't have tears in my eyes for you, but I've got tears in my voice. It breaks my heart—the thought that if death seized upon you tonight, you'd end up in Hell. So, I'll be praying for you and thinking about you, and hope you'll give serious thought to your eternal salvation. So, thanks for talking to me, Josh, I really appreciate it.

JOSH: Thank you so much. That was a *really* great conversation, I appreciated it.

CHAPTER SIX

MORE SIGNS OF THE TIMES

> knowing this first: that scoffers will come in the last days, walking according to their own lusts, and saying, "Where is the promise of His coming?"

THE BELOW PORTION of Scripture gives us additional signs that would be evident when we are living in the "last days."

> But know this, that in the last days perilous times will come: For men will be lovers of themselves, lovers of money, boasters, proud, blasphemers, disobedient to parents, unthankful, unholy, unloving, unforgiving, slanderers, without self-control, brutal, despisers of good, traitors, headstrong, haughty, lovers of pleasure rather than lovers of God, having a form of godliness but denying its power. And from such people turn away! (2 Timothy 3:1–5)

These are some of the signs that indicate the time in which we live:

"Perilous times will come." Who could argue that we aren't living in perilous times? Modern life is *inordinately* stressful. The worldwide pandemic killed many and the forced shutdown and stay-at-home orders crashed economies, causing vast numbers of Americans to consider the drastic step of taking their own lives. A CDC survey found that in June 2020, *11 percent of Americans seriously considered committing suicide* in the past thirty days, including one in four young adults ages eighteen to twenty-

four.[23] Eleven percent of the US population translates to over twenty-five million human beings!

In 2020, life, with all its stresses, suddenly became unbearably miserable. Millions of people were stripped of much of its pleasure and were confined to their homes without income or the ability to visit family and friends. It's understandable that a godless generation that has been incessantly taught they are mere primates with no rhyme or reason to live would consider ending it all.

Without the fear of God, which the Bible says is the "beginning of wisdom" (Proverbs 9:10), Scripture tells us that in the last days people would be lovers of themselves. We don't have to look far to see that we are the generation of selfishness. We are concerned about looks, bank accounts, our rights, our ego, and our personal happiness more than the happiness of others. When someone does something kind for another person, it often finds its way onto the national news. That a human being was kind becomes "remarkable," in the truest sense of the word.

Read or watch the news tonight, and you won't need too much convincing that this generation of proud boasters, who blaspheme God's name without the slightest fear, fit the bill. The other signs given by Scripture certainly have become more prevalent in recent years. People would increasingly be:

- Lovers of money
- Disobedient to parents
- Unthankful
- Unholy
- Unloving
- Unforgiving
- Slanderers
- Without self-control
- Brutal
- Despisers of good
- Traitors
- Headstrong
- Haughty
- Lovers of pleasure rather than lovers of God
- Having a form of godliness without its power

These traits will naturally manifest the works of the flesh:

> Now the works of the flesh are evident, which are: adultery, fornication, uncleanness, lewdness, idolatry, sorcery, hatred, contentions, jealousies, outbursts of wrath, selfish ambitions, dissensions, heresies, envy, murders, drunkenness, revelries, and the like; of which I tell you beforehand, just as I also told you in time past, that those who practice such things will not inherit the kingdom of God. (Galatians 5:19–21)

But when the gospel makes its entrance, it transforms us. The works of the flesh are replaced with the fruit of the Spirit:

> But the fruit of the Spirit is love, joy, peace, longsuffering, kindness, goodness, faithfulness, gentleness, self-control. Against such there is no law. (Galatians 5:22,23)

Of course, these twenty "signs" of the last days have *always* been around. There hasn't been a time in human history when people weren't proud, blasphemous, boastful, disobedient to parents, etc., but in the end times these will become far more prevalent. Look at how specific Scripture is about why the ungodly would scoff at these being signs of the end of the age:

> Beloved, I now write to you this second epistle (in both of which I stir up your pure minds by

way of reminder), that you may be mindful of the words which were spoken before by the holy prophets, and of the commandment of us, the apostles of the Lord and Savior, knowing this first: that scoffers will come in the last days, *walking according to their own lusts*, and saying, "Where is the promise of His coming? For since the fathers fell asleep, all things continue as they were from the beginning of creation." For this they willfully forget: that by the word of God the heavens were of old, and the earth standing out of water and in the water, by which the world that then existed perished, being flooded with water. But the heavens and the earth which are now preserved by the same word, are reserved for fire until the day of judgment and perdition of ungodly men.

But, beloved, do not forget this one thing, that with the Lord one day is as a thousand years, and a thousand years as one day. The Lord is not slack concerning His promise, as some count slackness, *but is longsuffering toward us, not willing that any should perish but that all should come to repentance.*

But the day of the Lord will come as a thief in the night, in which the heavens will pass away with a great noise, and the elements will melt with fervent heat; both the earth and the works that are in it will be burned up. Therefore, since all these things will be dissolved, what manner of persons ought you to be in holy conduct and godliness, looking for and hastening the coming of the day of God, because of which the heavens will be dissolved, being on fire, and the elements will melt with fervent heat? Nevertheless we, according to His promise, look for new heavens and a new earth in which righteousness dwells. (2 Peter 3:1–13)

People "willingly forget: that . . . the world that then existed perished, being flooded with water" (verses 5,6). Many today deny there was a worldwide flood that destroyed most of humanity. According to these verses, those who scoff at these signs, believing that God would not send a judgment for sin, do so because they are given to lust. And the reason God hasn't sent death to arrest them is that He is patiently waiting for them to repent.

There are many prophecies of the Bible which we haven't studied, mainly because there is contention —not about their authenticity, but about their timeline. We will look at some of the less contentious signs in our final chapter.

CHAPTER SEVEN

THEN THE END
WILL COME

AS IT
WAS IN THE
DAYS OF
NOAH, SO
WILL IT BE
AT THE
COMING OF
THE SON OF
MAN

THE BIBLE TELLS US to be on the lookout for a few more signs of the end times. Here are additional indicators that we are in the "latter times."

Interest in the Occult

Now the Spirit expressly says that in latter times some will depart from the faith, giving heed to deceiving spirits and doctrines of demons... (1 Timothy 4:1)

As Josh sat on the picnic bench in the local park, he was fulfilling Bible prophecy through his fascination with the forbidden arts. Millions give themselves to "doctrines of demons" as they delve into the dark

69

side of horoscopes, Ouija boards, tarot cards, satanism, séances, etc.

But there is another aspect to these verses. The Scriptures repeatedly warn against apostasy, as people fall prey to false teachers and depart from the Christian faith. "Doctrines of demons" includes the deceptive teaching heard in many churches today that pervert the Bible. Many professing Christians compromise with the sinful world. They have a form of godliness, but they lack the power of God in their lives. The prevalence of religious hypocrisy is undeniable, and is a sad indication of the end times.

Interest in Vegetarianism

> Now the Spirit expressly says that in latter times some will depart from the faith,... commanding to abstain from foods which God created to be received with thanksgiving by those who believe and know the truth. For every creature of God is good, and nothing is to be refused if it is received with thanksgiving. (1 Timothy 4:1,3,4)

God bless those folks who love animals, but there are still millions who love them juicy and tender. I love animals and could have easily been swayed into vegetarianism. But God made certain animals to be eaten, so we can enjoy a good steak without any guilt.

In the story of the Prodigal Son, Jesus didn't say to kill the fatted cabbage. He said to kill the fatted calf (see Luke 15:23) and rejoice in celebration. Whatever the case, the interest in vegetarianism is a sign that we are living in the days just before the coming of Christ.

Corruption and Violence

> But as the days of Noah were, so also will the coming of the Son of Man be. For as in the days before the flood, they were eating and drinking, marrying and giving in marriage, until the day that Noah entered the ark, and did not know until the flood came and took them all away, so also will the coming of the Son of Man be. (Matthew 24:37–39)

According to Genesis 6:11, this was what was happening during that particular time: "The earth also was corrupt before God, and the earth was filled with violence."

Who could argue against the fact that in recent years society has become increasingly corrupt and violent? We have seen corruption in politics, in business, in government, among the police—in almost every sphere of society, people are more than willing to break the law. Our cities have become war zones, where violence, mass shootings, and murder have become commonplace.

The Most Important Sign

Jesus spoke of another event that would happen in the last days—the most important one. He said the gospel will be preached throughout the world before the end comes:

> "And this gospel of the kingdom will be preached in all the world as a witness to all the nations, and then the end will come." (Matthew 24:14)

This shows that God is rich in mercy. The glorious gospel—in which He promises everlasting life to all who repent and trust Jesus—will be preached as a witness to all nations. For two thousand years missionaries have put their lives in jeopardy to take the gospel to foreign lands, and this insignificant little book you're reading has played a small part in that Great Commission, which began when Jesus said,

> "Go into all the world and preach the gospel to every creature. He who believes and is

baptized will be saved; but he who does not believe will be condemned." (Mark 16:15,16)

We are nearing the time when the door of mercy will soon be closed. Don't put off your eternal salvation—not only because God may close the door in our lifetime, but because death could seize upon you tonight. So make sure you get right with God today.

Look at how fearful it will be when Jesus comes:

> . . . since it is a righteous thing with God to repay with tribulation those who trouble you, and to give you who are troubled rest with us when the Lord Jesus is revealed from heaven with His mighty angels, in flaming fire taking vengeance on those who do not know God, and on those who do not obey the gospel of our Lord Jesus Christ. These shall be punished with everlasting destruction from the presence of the Lord and from the glory of His power, when He comes, in that Day, to be glorified in His saints and to be admired among all those who believe, because our testimony among you was believed. (2 Thessalonians 1:6–10)

Final Thoughts

We have briefly looked at several evidences that we are living in the last days. You, of course, are free not to be convinced. However, I hope you *are* convinced—not because I want to persuade you concerning prophecy, but because I want (like the apostle Paul) to persuade you concerning Jesus.

We have looked at both the Prophets and the Law of Moses. Remember, the Prophets establish the credibility of Scripture. My hope is that you have seen that for the Scriptures to contain such clear prophecies, they *must* have been inspired by God. The Law, however, brings the knowledge of sin, and reveals that we are guilty sinners in terrible danger. It shows us that the Grim Reaper is justified in cutting us down through death, and that the Law will justly damn us if we cling to our sins.

My hope is that, because of both the Law and the Prophets, you see your need of His mercy. Please, right now, repent and put your trust in Jesus.

When Nathan the prophet exposed the sin of King David, this was the king's earnest prayer (make this prayer your own):

Have mercy upon me, O God,
According to Your lovingkindness;
According to the multitude of Your tender
    mercies,
Blot out my transgressions.
Wash me thoroughly from my iniquity,
And cleanse me from my sin.

For I acknowledge my transgressions,
And my sin is always before me.
Against You, You only, have I sinned,
And done this evil in Your sight—

That You may be found just when You speak,
And blameless when You judge.

Behold, I was brought forth in iniquity,
And in sin my mother conceived me.
Behold, You desire truth in the inward parts,
And in the hidden part You will make me to
    know wisdom.

Purge me with hyssop, and I shall be clean;
Wash me, and I shall be whiter than snow.
Make me hear joy and gladness,
That the bones You have broken may rejoice.
Hide Your face from my sins,
And blot out all my iniquities.

Create in me a clean heart, O God,
And renew a steadfast spirit within me.
(Psalm 51:1–10)

Now trust Jesus for your eternal salvation, read the Bible daily, and obey what you read.

These Perilous Times

As we have seen, Jesus warned that the time would come when men's hearts would fail them for fear of the things coming upon the earth (see Luke 21:26). No doubt when Jerusalem was besieged in AD 70, men's hearts failed them as the enemy entered the city. And in more modern times those without a living faith in God are susceptible to the torments of fear.

These *are* perilous times. Therefore, keep your eyes on Jesus. When you see these things begin to happen, He said to look up, because our redemption is drawing near (see Luke 21:28). We have nothing to fear but a lack of faith—because a lack of faith in God automatically defaults to fear. Trust in your faithful Creator, and rest in Him.

Psalm 46 begins with this bold statement:

God is our refuge and strength,
A very present help in trouble. (verse 1)

The Bible doesn't say that God *was* our refuge and strength. Or He *will be*. He *is* our refuge and strength. And He's not just our refuge—a place to hide in the storm—but He is our *strength*. With Him by our side, we are not weak and trembling. Nor is He merely a "help" in trouble, nor a "present help" in trouble. He is a "*very* present help" in trouble. As a loving and concerned Father, He has us by the hand.

The Scriptures then say,

Therefore we will not fear, even though the earth be removed, and though the mountains be carried into the midst of the sea... (Psalm 46:2)

What a glorious hope we have for the future:

And I heard a loud voice from heaven saying, "Behold, the tabernacle of God is with men, and He will dwell with them, and they shall be His people. God Himself will be with them and be their God. And God will wipe away every tear from their eyes; there shall be no more death, nor sorrow, nor crying. There shall be no more pain, for the former things have passed away." (Revelation 21:3,4)

Like a little child whose birthday is approaching, those who trust in Jesus are counting the days.

NOTES

1. "How many atoms are in the human body?" JLab Science Education <education.jlab.org/qa/mathatom_04.html>.
2. Kate Lohnes, "Siege of Jerusalem," *Encyclopaedia Britannica* <britannica.com/event/Siege-of-Jerusalem-70>.
3. David Guzik, "Matthew 24 – Jesus' Olivet Discourse," 2018, Enduring Word <enduringword.com/bible-commentary/matthew-24/>.
4. Owen Jarus, "Ancient Israel: A Brief History," August 16, 2016, Live Science <livescience.com/55774-ancient-israel.html>.
5. "A Restored Israel and Jewish Jerusalem," Jewish Voice <jewishvoice.org/learn/restored-israel-and-jewish-jerusalem>.
6. "Facts About Israel: History," 2010, Israel's Ministry of Foreign Affairs <tinyurl.com/yymwtwmu>.
7. "Arab-Israeli wars," *Encyclopaedia Britannica* <britannica.com/event/Arab-Israeli-wars>.
8. Chris Mitchell, "'The Temple Mount Is In Our Hands': The Words That Still Shake Israel 53 Years Later," June 3, 2020, CBN News <tinyurl.com/y67e8q65>.
9. "A Restored Israel and Jewish Jerusalem," Jewish Voice <tinyurl.com/y5yzva7w>.
10. Dr. Herbert Hillel Goldberg, "Jerusalem—A Burdensome Stone," Lema'an Zion <hashivah.org/jerusalem-a-burden-some-stone/>.
11. Steven M. Collins, "Jerusalem Becoming a Modern 'Burden-some Stone for all People,'" January 16, 2017 <tinyurl.com/y92exynn>.
12. Dr. J. Vernon McGee, "Armageddon: What? Where? When?" Blue Letter Bible <tinyurl.com/ya2yk43w>.

13. Jordan Strandness, "Why is the Israel-Palestine Conflict So Hard to Resolve?" February 5, 2019, The Rest of the Iceberg <tinyurl.com/y8p75hmk>.

14. Jayson Casper, "Can 'Abraham' Bring Peace to the Middle East?" August 17, 2020, *Christianity Today* <tinyurl.com/yatwqgk3>.

15. "Trump announces 'peace deal' between Bahrain and Israel," September 11, 2020, *BBC News* <bbc.com/news/world-middle-east-54124996>.

16. Mark Landler, "Another Gulf State Recognizes Israel. Here's Why It Matters," September 12, 2020, *The New York Times* <tinyurl.com/y3klv47z>.

17. Owen Amos, "Why do US evangelicals support Trump's Jerusalem policy?" January 5, 2018, *BBC News* <bbc.com/news/world-us-canada-42402350>.

18. Charles Spurgeon, "The Church of Christ" delivered on June 3, 1855 at New Park Street Chapel, Southward; quoted on *The Jerusalem Connection Report* <tinyurl.com/ychfbeq9>.

19. Benjamin Gurrentz, "Living with an Unmarried Partner Now Common for Young Adults," November 15, 2018, U.S. Census Bureau <tinyurl.com/ydalwj5n>.

20. Mark A. Michaels and Patricia Johnson, "Is Traditional Marriage On Its Way Out?" Dec. 1, 2015, *PRNewswire* <tinyurl.com/y55azl67>.

21. Romans 1:26, *New Defender's Study Bible* <icr.org/bible/Romans/1/26/>.

22. Thomas Watson, "The Epistle to the Reader," *The Doctrine of Repentance* (1668).

23. "Mental Health, Substance Use, and Suicidal Ideation During the COVID-19 Pandemic—United States, June 24–30, 2020," *Morbidity and Mortality Weekly Report (MMWR)*, August 14, 2020, CDC <cdc.gov/mmwr/volumes/69/wr/mm6932a1.htm>.

RESOURCES

If you have not yet placed your trust in Jesus Christ and would like additional information, please check out the following helpful resources:

How to Know God Exists. Clear evidences for His existence will convince you that belief in God is reasonable and rational—a matter of fact and not faith.

The Evidence Bible. Answers to over 200 questions, thousands of comments, and 130 informative articles will help you better comprehend the Christian faith.

Why Christianity? (DVD). If you have ever asked what happens after we die, if there is a Heaven, or how good we have to be to go there, this DVD will help you.

See our YouTube channel (youtube.com/livingwaters) to watch free movies such as "The Atheist Delusion," "Evolution vs. God," "Crazy Bible," as well as thousands of other fascinating videos.

If you are a new believer, please read *Save Yourself Some Pain*, written just for you (available free online at LivingWaters.com, or as a booklet).

For more resources, visit **LivingWaters.com**, call 800-437-1893, or write to: Living Waters Publications, P.O. Box 1172, Bellflower, CA 90707.

RAY COMFORT is a bestselling author who has written more than 90 books. He also cohosts a television program that airs in over 190 countries and is an award-winning filmmaker whose movies have been seen by millions.

He and his wife, Sue, live in Southern California and have three grown children.